Vacation Bible School

Cinderella's best friend is Amazing

Workbook
& Coloring
book
With
Devotions
Dramas
& Art

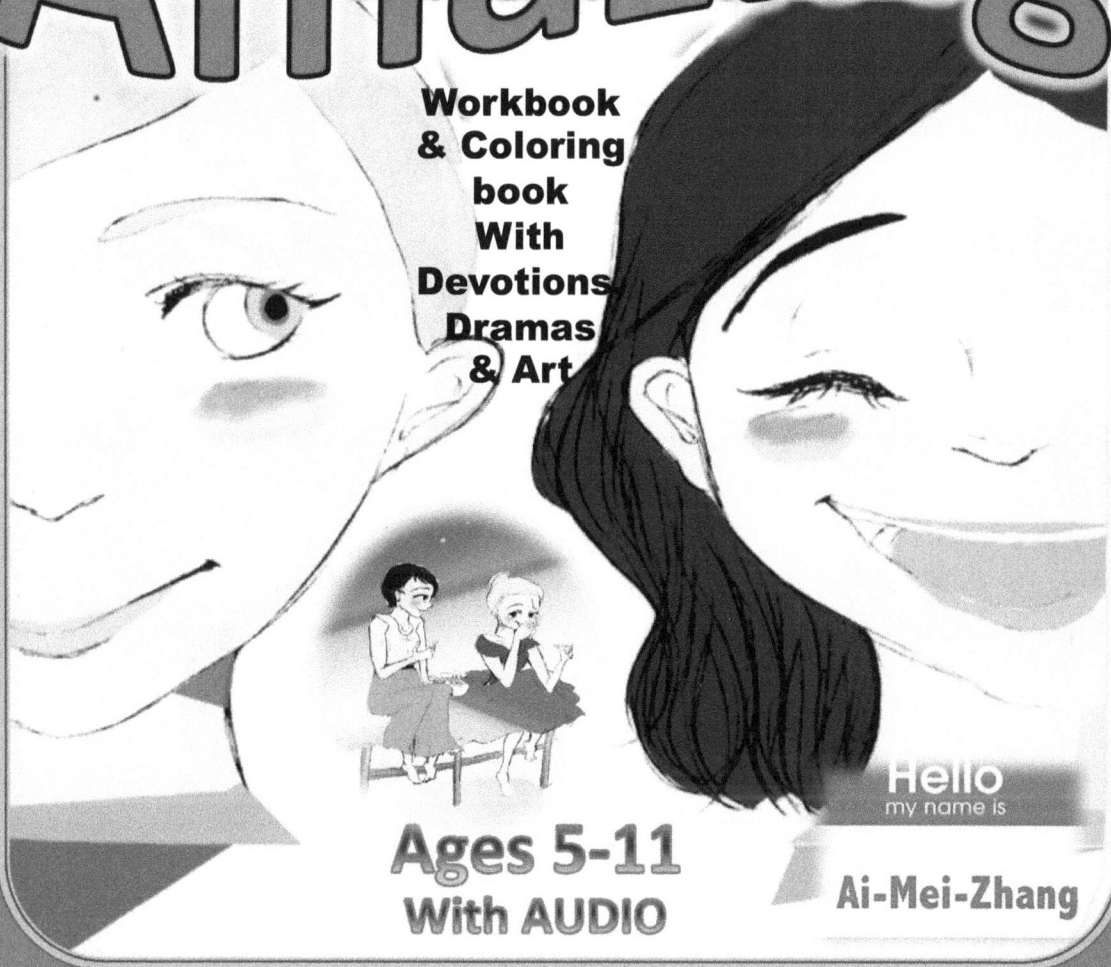

Ages 5-11
With AUDIO

Hello
my name is

Ai-Mei-Zhang

By Tamilla Palmer Perera

Vacation Bible School

Cinderella's best friend is Amazing

Workbook & Coloring book With Devotions, Dramas & Art

Ages 5-11
With AUDIO

Hello
my name is
Ai-Mei-Zhang

By Tamilla Palmer Perera

Published January 1, 2017

12 Streams Encouragement Center
12secs.com

For copies or speaking engagements, go to Amazon.com or

contact info@12secs.com

Other Books by Tamilla and Asela Perera

Daddy Love Letters: Jeremy Meets His Two Fathers
Cinderella's Best Friend is Amazing (Chinese)
Four Spicy Christmases
12 Seconds for Manifesting Your Blessings for Dates, Marriage and Finances
Cinderella Asela

Read to Students at the Beginning of the First Class - The story of Cinderella is amazing and we all love it for different reasons but it was only a fairy tale. Yet in the Bible in the Book of Daniel 4:3, it says of God, "His kingdom is an everlasting kingdom and his dominion is from generation to generation." Therefore, God is telling us that there is another kingdom to consider that is far larger, much longer lasting and totally real... the Kingdom of God. Let us see how the story Cinderella's Best Friend is Amazing relates to the Kingdom of God in this highly unique Vacation Bible School Curriculum.

Why we chose this theme: Cinderella…

Actually, we were praying and the Holy Spirit gave us the whole story in 1 hour.

Preface to this VBS Study

- A name can become a synonymous of an action.

- For example some people have become so famous that their names are like actions

- Sherwin is know for paint

- Steve Jobs for Apple

- Arnold Palmer for golfing

- By understanding God's Names better, students can become closer to God.

- God is so serious about helping us that He actually reveals His special names in the Bible which relate to our specific needs.

> This book is also designed to give students practice with English comprehension which will greatly increase their ability to understand the spiritual lessons in the devotions.

Table of Contents

Sample VBS Order of Curriculum Usage

- 1st – Songtime/Worship

Use Your own or Learn the Song in this book.

Challenge Students with the themes on the Table of Contents. VBS Book

- 2nd – Devotion

Best combined with Song-Time. VBS Book

The Book formats are all available as E=books.

- 3rd – Arts & Craft

Be careful to do these prior to the skit it complements.

These are located in the Skit book.

- 4th – Skits

Use these for preschoolers and younger ages especially.

Also, good for older ages. Skit book.

- 5th – Workbook Activities

Use these as homework or in the free time. VBS Book

HIGHLY RECOMMENDED – Throw a party/ball at the end of the curriculum on the last day to invite parents and perform the key scenes

Theme Song – Day by Day
(audio supplied free in kit)
Original Lyrics by
Tamilla Palmer Perera

Day by Day

Hour by Hour

Minute by Minute, Lord

Show us your Power

You will come to bless us

You will come to show us (repeat)

Your great, great love

Your great, great love

LESSON 1: FRIENDSHIP!

Draw a picture of you and your best friend.

Once upon a time,
on a beautiful sunny day
two friends sat side by side.
One girl was known as
Cinderella and she was British.
The other girl was named
Amazing and she was Chinese.
They loved to hang out at the
brink of the river eating
pumpkin seeds and throwing
stones into the water.

This story is continued in Cinderella's Best Friend is
Amazing, E-book or Printed Book

Directions: Color us in! Tell a partner what colors you used and why.

Lesson 1 – True friends are great!

Key Vocabulary

Column A	Column B/Synonyms	Column C/Antonyms
1. Sat	a. body of water	A. from America
2. Was	b. rocks	b. land
3. Hang out	c. edge	C. keep
4. Eat	d. in the past	D. specks
5. Throw	e. perch	E. numerous
6. Brink	f. one time	F. go deep
7. Stones	g. have fun together	G. is
8. British	h. toss	H. stand
9. River	i. chew	i. bored
10. Once	j. from England	J. Drink

Insert the right word from column A into a sentence below:

1. The _____ people are known to be polite.

2. Don't _____ trash into the streets.

3. When you sit at the _____ of the river, you can see your face in the water.

4. Sticks and _____ may break my bones, but words will never hurt me.

5. Only _____ with people that you know well.

6. Your mother _____ your best friend when you were born.

7. Do not lie to a fiend even _____.

8. The girl _____ down and her chair broke because it was too small.

9. _____ health foods, not fat foods.

10. A _____ may contain crocodiles and alligators.

Lesson 1

Comprehension Quiz/Discussion Questions

Directions: Students should copy the questions from below onto a sheet of paper and answer them in groups of two or by themselves. Then discuss as a large group.

1. Who is Cinderella?
2. How is she different from Amazing?
3. Where are they sitting?
4. What are they eating?.
5. What boyish hobby do like to do?
6. Do you think the girls are tomboys?
7. How do you know they are or aren't tomboys?
8. What is the weather like?
9. What kind of hairstyle are the girls wearing?
10. What year is it?

1. She is a British princess who is most likely an orphan
2. She is British whereas her friend is Chinese
3. At the brink of a river
4. Pumkin seeds which are good for the heart.
5. Throwing stones in the water
6. No
7. because they are wearing dresses, nor shorts or pants
8. Sunny which means everything is going great so far.
9. Cinderella is wearing a bun and her friend is wearing a short bob haircut.
10. It is unknown, but it is a long long time ago as hinted by once upon a time

Dialogue- She loves to share!

Cinderella: Oh boy, throwing those stones into the water has really made me hungry.

Amazing: Me too!

Cinderella: Let's see! I've got some pumpkin seeds here.

Amazing: Can you share with me?

Cinderella: Of course! There's enough for two people.

Amazing: Thank you so much!

Discussion 1/Journal Questions

Who are your closest friends? Why?

_____

_____

_____

_____

_____

Is Jesus Christ one of your friends? Why or why not?

_____

_____

_____

_____

_____

DEVOTION: Friendship and the Friend of Sinners
Why you need a friend that is closer than a brother

Lesson #1 – Friendship –Just like Amazing and Cinderella were great friends, so we can also be great friends with God. But friendship only happens through asking Jesus Christ to forgive our sins and wrongs because God hates sin. Since God is Holy and He hates sin, the only access to heaven and a friendlier relationship with God is by asking Jesus Christ to come into your heart. In Matthew 19:11, Jesus Christ was known as a friend of sinners. God wants to be your friend today!

Think about this Theme: <u>Access to the Kingdom of God comes through friendship with Jesus Christ first.</u>

1. Isaiah 59:1 (No one can be close to God who loves being bad and doing the wrong thing) But your iniquities have separated between **you** and your God, and **your sins** have **hid his face from you**, that he will not hear.

2. Habakkuk 1:13 (No one can be close to God who is full of evil and sin) (God) You are too pure with your eyes than to look on evil

3. John 15:14 (No one can be close to God if they refuse to obey him) **You** are My friends if **you do** what I command **you**

4. John 15:13(No one can be close to God if they don't understand that Jesus died for them) **Greater love hath no man than this, that a man** lay down his life for his friends.

5. John 3:16 (No one can be close to God if they don't believe him) For God so loved the world that he gave his one and only Son, that whoever believes in him shall not perish but have eternal life.

6. Ephesians 2:15 (No one can be close to God if they believe God is their enemy) He tore down the wall we used to keep us away…

Summary: God wants to be close to us. We have to decide to be close to Him.

CHILD TESTIMONY

Why you need a friend that is closer than a brother

When I was 8 years old, I was a fighter. Though I am a female, I usually fought boys. This was really strange because I was an A student but I had a temper. Whenever someone would say something to me that I did not like, I would say, "Do you want to fight about it?" Then I would ball up my fists and give the meanest look I could which was usually one eye poked out.

Not wanting to be the one to start the fight, I would wait until the first punch slowing rotating around my enemy in a circle. I remember my third grade teacher saying of me and another student, "Look at them. They look like two chickens." If the other person hit me, I would definitely hit him back. But one day while I was at church, I heard my youth pastor say, "Children be careful! Right now you are under grace because you don't know any better. But you can get to an age of responsibility where God will say you're old enough to know better." I thought about his words and knew that he was talking to me because even though I wanted to be a nice person, I considered myself a bad girl, a mean girl.

Then one day three of my friends, the Walker Boys, went swimming in the Mississippi River. The riptide was very heavy that day and only two boys came out. My friend Peanut died. The following Sunday the youth pastor asked all children to come into the sanctuary for a special meeting. He said, "Remember what I told you about the age of responsibility. Peanut died because he was a disobedient boy. It's time for you children to respond to the Bible and to accept Jesus Christ into your hearts. I was so afraid, I decided right then and there, I was going to accept Jesus and ask him to forgive me for sins. I prayed and immediately the heart of meanness I had disappeared. I was so changed that my third grade teacher asked me to be the Class Leader.

Life Application: Become the friend of Jesus today, come to Jesus. Romans 10:9-10
If you declare with your mouth, "Jesus is Lord," and believe in your heart that God raised him from the dead, you will be saved. For it is with your heart that you believe and are justified, and it is with your mouth that you profess your faith and are saved.

Drama: (Students can make up their own skit)
Characters: God, Angel Doorkeeper, Good-doer
"Knock knock , may I see God." "Sorry, he is not available. Unless you're coming with Jesus you are not permitted to come in."

LESSON 2: My Stuff

Draw a picture of your favorite thing.

Directions: Color my towel just like your towel at home

Picture B

Lesson 2 – Amazing Loses Her Favorite Thing

Key Vocabulary

Column A	Column B/Synonyms	Column C/Antonyms
1. Head	a. sea	A. Hold on
2. Swim	b. buddy	b. Walk
3. Drop	c. go in	C. bully
4. Ran	d. wade	D. sand
5. Find	e. cover n.	E. outside
6. Beach	f. quickly returning	F. nakedness
7. Cottage	g. house	G. wait
8. towel	h. Release	H. stand still
9. Right back!	i. look for	i. inside
10. Friend	j. sprinted	J. forget about

Insert the right word from column A into a sentence below:

1. What would happen if two people _____ in the door at the same time?

2. If someone does not know how to _____, don't push them into the pool.

3. If someone _____ something, a nice thing to do is to pick it up.

4. The Big Bad Wolf _____ after Goldilocks.

5. If you _____ a coin, it's best to give it back to the owner.

6. When you go to the _____, don't get burned.

7. A _____ doesn't look exactly like a house.

8. Use a _____ to wipe up drops from washing your hair.

9. If you promise someone that you will be _____, do not wait around.

10. A _____ is more known by kind actions not big words.

Lesson 2

Comprehension Quiz/Discussion Questions

Directions: Students should copy the questions from below onto a sheet of paper and answer them in groups of two or by themselves. Then discuss as a large group.

1. What did Amazing forget?
2. Where did she leave it?
3. Why did she need her towel?
4. What was gross?
5. What is a tadpole?
6. What did Cinderella think about the tadpole?
7. Why did the girls dislike the tadpole?
8. What was Amazing going to do to clean off Cinderella's leg?
9. Did Cinderella try to help her?
10. Why did Amazing forget the towel?

1. Her beach towel
2. Probably on the floor
3. To wipe off her leg
4. The black tadpole
5. The black tadpole
6. Gross! It was gross!
7. Because it was sticking to her which means it was hard to get off of her.
8. Get her towel so that she could wipe off her leg
9. Yes, Cinderella was being friendly. She was looking around for it.
10. She was a little careless. She should have remembered it.

Dialogue- Get it off!

Directions: Practice saying underlined words out loud. Do dialogue in groups of two. Then have two people act it out in front of class.

Amazing: Look, a tadpole is on your foot.

Cinderella: That's gross! Quick, get it off!

Amazing: I know! Where is my towel?

Cinderella: I don't see it. Oh, here, you can use mine.

(Amazing cleaned the tiny frog off)

Cinderella: Oh, thank you! I really owe you for that one!

Amazing: I'll be right back!

I must have left my towel in the cottage.

Discussion 2/ Journal Questions

What is your favorite thing?

_____

Have you ever lost it?

_____

How does your family members treat you when you lose something precious?

_____

Do you have anything precious inside of you that you can't lose?

_____

What is it? How do you know you can't lose it?

_____

Why does God value us so much? Do you believe you are precious?

_____

_____

DEVOTION 2: The Heavenly Father

Why God thinks you're precious

Lesson #2 – My Things/My Stuff – Just like Cinderella valued Amazing, so God values everyone. It's very easy to look at someone who is having a hard year and to think that person is no good. Many people think that a person is "bye bye" if one of their teeth is broken or they have dirty clothes or they were in jail. If we think so poorly about these people, what do we think about Jesus who was kicked out of his home, stripped of his clothes and totally beaten up. But God values all of us because He created us. He is a good, good Father!

Think about the Theme: <u>People are the jewels of the Kingdom</u> because the Heavenly Father thinks we are precious.

1. Matthew 10:31 (God says we are of more value) Therefore don't be afraid. **You are of more value than** many **sparrows.**

2. Malachi 3:17 (God says that we are a special treasure) And they shall be to me a special treasure, says Jehovah of hosts, in the day that I prepare; and I will spare them as a man spares his own son that serves him.

3. Deuteronomy 7:7-8 (God says that he has set his loves on us) The LORD did not set his love upon you, nor choose you, because ye were more ... **but because the LORD loved you** and kept the oath which He swore to your fathers**...**

Summary: God has a loving heart and wants us to learn how to have the same kind of heart towards all kinds of people. This does not mean that we are dumb and hang out with dangerous people. It just means that we think everyone has a high value, no matter how they look or what they have done. No one is to be thrown out with the trash.

Child Testimony

When we moved into our new three bedroom home in the valley, we were so happy. We loved the clean street and nice neighbors. But there was an old woman across the street who had many children living with her. But they were not the kind of children we could play with. They were different. We asked our mother, "Why do those children walk funny or have hands that look broken or have one eye closed?" My mother said, "Don't ever tease them. They are good people just like you are they just had some kind of accident in their lives." Therefore, whenever we saw them, we always waved and smiled at them. One day one of the girls asked if we would like to come over and play. We crossed the street and had a really good time. Their mother was so happy that one day she came over to our house to give us presents. She told my mom, "Your children are the only ones on this whole street who treat my children kindly and I appreciate them. I just wanted to bring them some toys to thank them for playing with my children."

Drama: Recognize your value and value in others:
Actors: God and You
Go to God and say, "You love because of my age, my background, my As, my goodness, and my awesome family."
God says, "No, I love u because I just want to."

Life Application: Bring lunch or a snack for a student who has been mistreated.

Songtime: Activity: Think about if there is anyone you see as less valuable than a king or queen. Ask yourself why do I believe that and what have I learned today.

LESSON 3: FAMILY
Draw a picture of your family.

Picture C

Directions: Color in the person who is the happiest.

Lesson 3

Comprehension Quiz/Discussion Questions

Directions: Students should copy the questions from below onto a sheet of paper and answer them in groups of two or by themselves. Then discuss as a large group.

1. In what room was Cinderella's mom?
2. What did she do to Amazing's hand?
3. Does she like Amazing?
4. Is she Amazing's real mom?
5. Why was Amazing called an addition?
6. What did she ask Amazing to promise?
7. Why did Amazing run from the room?
8. Is Cinderella's mom sick?
9. Is Amazing upset? How do you know that Amazing is upset?
10. Is Cinderella's mom upset?

1. The setting room
2. She grabbed it.
3. Yes because she calls her a lovely girl.
4. No.
5. Because she is her host mom
6. To take care of Cinderella
7. She was confused.
8. Yes
9. Yes, She asked herself a question. (have any of you ever asked yourself a ????)
10. Yes, but she seems kind of calm

Lesson 3 – Family

Key Vocabulary

Column A	Column B/Synonyms	Column C/Antonyms
1. lie	a. sea	A. to keep busy
2. See	b. buddy	b. ignore
3. Grab	c. comes near	C. loosen
4. Approaches	d. extra person	D. sand
5. Great	e. relative.	E. outside
6. Addition	f. not well	F. healthy
7. Sick	g. spy out	G. waiting around
8. lovely	h. wonderful	H. rejection
9. Family	i. grasp	i. Stupid
10. Promise	j. rest	J. stranger

Insert the right word from column A into a sentence below:

1. When you _____ down for bed, you should shower first.

2. Never make a _____ that you don't plan to keep.

3. If someone _____ that you don't know, don't go with them.

4. A _____ member should always try to help one another.

5. If you are _____, do not shake hands with others.

6. When someone offers you a treat, do not _____it, wait for them to put it in your hand.

7. A _____ person has good manners.

8. If you _____a student fall, you would help them up.

9. Good is better than okay and _____ is better than good.

10. A new _____ was added to our family.

Dialogue- I promise!

Cinderella's Mom: Amazing, come quickly!

Amazing: Yes...

Cinderella's Mom: "Amazing! Lovely girl! You've been a great addition to our family.

Amazing: Huh...

Cinderella's Mom: I'm sick and dying now.

Amazing: Oh no...

Cinderella's Mom: You must promise me that you'll look after Cinderella after I'm gone."

Amazing: Yes! I promise.

Discussion 3/Journal Questions

Who's family do you belong to?

_____

_____

_____

_____

How did you become a part of that family?

_____

_____

_____

_____

Who looks after you? Do they do a good job?

_____

_____

Is anyone here in the family of God? What do you think
of that family?

_____

_____

DEVOTION 3: Family and the God who is with us

What it means to be added to God's family

Lesson #3 – Family – Just like Amazing became a part of Cinderella's family, so God wants us to be a part of His family because He is with us. To become a member of God's family does not mean that you become God. But it does mean that your identity will change. Not only do you become a friend of God, but you also become a son or daughter of the King. In 2 Corinthians 6:17 Message Bible, God says, "Don't link up with those who pollute you. I want you all to myself. I'll be a father to you and you will be sons and daughters to me.'

Think about this Theme: <u>There is a Kingdom family</u>.

1. Ephesians 4:5-6 (Before man was ever made, there was a God known as Father) There is **One Lord**, **one faith**, **one** baptism, One **God** and Father of all, who is above all, and through all, and in you all.

2. John 1:1 (Before man was ever made, there was already a kingdom family) **In the beginning was the Word, and the Word was with God, and the Word was God**. The same was in the beginning with God.

3. Ephesians 1:56 (Before man was ever made, God already loved us and planned for us to be in His family.) How blessed is God! And what a blessing he is! He's the Father of our Master, Jesus Christ, and takes us to the high places of blessing in him. Long before he laid down earth's foundations, he had us in mind, had settled on us as the focus of his love, to be made whole and holy by his love. Long, long ago he decided to adopt us into his family through Jesus Christ. (What pleasure he took in planning this!) He wanted us to enter into the celebration of his lavish gift-giving by the hand of his beloved Son.

God's kingdom consists of the Heavenly Father, Jesus the Son, the Holy Spirit, numerous angels, and anyone who has asked Jesus into his or her heart. Someone once said that God's wife is Mary, but that's not true. Mary was married to Joseph, the Carpenter.

Child Testimony

I wanted the grape juice so I Became a part of god's family

Being a member of the church is important, even if you're only 8 years old. I was so happy after I asked Jesus Christ to come into my heart. He took me from being an angry little girl to being a nice person.

One of the things I loved to do the most was prayer. I remember hearing about three Jewish boys who prayed and God protected them. My Sunday School Teacher taught me that prayer is an important part of my life. So I decided that I would pray every night at the side of my bed even if I was tired and had been out all day. After a while, I had memorized my prayer and I would pray the same thing a lot or sometimes, pray a new prayer.

Although my prayers to the Heavenly Father were small and simple, God usually answered them. There are three prayers of mine which were really special to me as I grew up;
1. I prayed for sick woman to feel better and she instantly got better and others also.
2. I prayed for my family to live on the west side of town which was upper middleclass and eventually one day we moved there.
3. I prayed to go to USC, University of Southern California and God made a way for me to graduate there.

Seeing God answer prayer became so big in my life that I was put in leadership of World Vision International's Office of Prayer serving over 120 countries.

Drama: Become a member of God's family – Act out an adoption into the family of God.

Characters are God, Jesus, orphan, and the Adoption Agency Officer.
Students should create a scene in which an orphan is adopted into God's family because of Jesus.

Life Application: Pass out certificates and have students sign their name to commit they are a member of God's family or they can copy a statement from the board into the front of their Bibles.

LESSON 4: Alone

Draw a picture of the day you were by yourself but wanted other people around.

Directions: Color in the person who is a good friend.

Picture D

Lesson 4

Comprehension Quiz/Discussion Questions

Directions: Students should copy the questions from below onto a sheet of paper and answer them in groups of two or by themselves. Then discuss as a large group.

1. How did Cinderella come into the room?
2. What was happening to her mother?
3. What did her mother give her?
4. What were Cinderella's mom's last words?
5. What do those last words mean?
6. Where was Cinderella's mom going?
7. Why didn't Cinderella want her mom to go?
8. What did Amazing promise Cinderella?
9. Does Cinderella have a father?
10. How do you know it?

10. Because Amazing mentioned him.
9. Yes
8. You have me.
7. She wasn't ready.
6. To heaven
5. Don't be afraid of messes/problems
4. A princess is a success no matter what a mess she may be in
3. A hug
2. She was dying
1. Quickly

Lesson 4 – Cinderella has to deal with being left

Key Vocabulary

Column A	Column B/Synonyms	Column C/Antonyms
1. Hurriedly	a. stop	A. hurt
2. Just in time	b. move quickly	b. forget
3. Hug	c. father	C. late
4. Sigh	d. shake head	D. fail
5. Knelt	e. victory	E. not move head
6. Remember	f. come to mind	F. healthy
7. Success	g. make a sad sound	G. laugh
8. knod	h. bow down to feet	H. move slowly
9. Finish	i. on time	i. stand up
10. Papa	j. Embrace	J. stranger

Insert the right word from column A into a sentence below:

1. A real lady never rushes, but she moves gracefully and _____ .

2. The gentleman saved the young lady _____ before she was hurt.

3. Don't _____ very loudly or a fly may fly into your mouth.

4. _____is a great word for father if you love him very much.

5. The knight _____in front of the king and received honor.

6. _____ your dinner before you eat your dessert.

7. Give a good _____ of your head if you like what someone says.

8. If you _____a student fall, you would help them up.

9. Always _____ to thank a person who helps you.

10. Remember, a prince is a _____ even if he is in a mess.

Dialogue-Bye, Bye for Now!

Cinderella's Mom: Bye, bye, my girl! I am going to heaven now.

Cinderella: Oh, Mom, so soon...

Cinderella's Mom: Yes, my dear! Remember, a princess is always a success no matter what a mess she may be in!

Cinderella: But mom, you can't go, I won't have anyone....

Cinderella's Mom: looks sick and goes...

Amazing (giving her a hug): Yes, you will Cinderella. You'll have me and Papa.

Discussion 4/Journal Questions

When were you ever left alone?

_____

_____

_____

How did you survive?

_____

_____

_____

Does God ever leave us alone?

_____

_____

_____

Does God leave us alone when we need Him the most?

_____

_____

_____

DEVOTION 4: Alone but, God is
Available by the Holy Spirit
Why you don't ever have to be alone again

Lesson #4 - Alone – Just like Cinderella knew where to find her mother, so there are places where we can always find God. Sometimes when you lose a family member, you can feel so alone. You can feel like the person who loves you the most is no longer available. You can feel like the one you loved disappeared and is never coming back. But anyone who died believing in Jesus Christ is waiting for you in heaven. While you continue to live on the earth without them, God is always near you. As a member of his spiritual family, He never leaves you alone. In fact, there are also places where you can strongly sense His presence on the earth too because His name also means, The Lord is There (Jehovah Shammah) Ezek. 48:3.

Think about this Theme: <u>There are Kingdom territories or places to find God</u>. Places where God dwells.

1. Isaiah 66:1 (One of the special places where we can find God is heaven) Thus says the LORD: "**Heaven is my throne**, and the earth is my footstool; what is the house that you would build for me..."

2. Matthew 5:35 (One of the special places where we can find God is the earth) But I tell you not to swear at all: either by heaven, for it is God's throne; <u>or by the earth, for it is His footstool; or by Jerusalem, for it is the city of the great King.</u>

3. 1 Timothy 3:15 (One of the special places where we can find God is the church) ... behave thyself in the house of God, which is the church of the living God, the pillar and ground of the truth.

4. Psalm 87:2 (One of the special places where we can find God is Mount Zion , a hill in Jerusalem that is known for God's presence especially since David conquered it) His foundation is in the holy mountains. <u>The LORD loves the gates of Zion More than all the other dwelling places of Jacob.</u> Glorious things are spoken of you, O city of God. Selah....

Child Testimony

The church is a place for everyone to be involved. When I was 7, I used to admire the children at my church. I saw them serving as junior ushers, singing in the choir, competing for Bible quizzes and partaking in the Lord's supper. One day I reached out my hand to have the cup of juice, but my older sister pinched me. She said, "You have not asked Jesus Christ into your heart yet. Children here are not welcome to the Lord's Supper unless they are baptized."

I was so disappointed. It made me want to suck my thumb. But shortly after that, the preacher asked the children at church, "Who here wants to become a child of God". My heart was beating fast. Would God accept me? I saw my older brother stand up and then my older sister. They had tears in their eyes and they were very emotional. I did not feel that emotion, but I felt scared. In my mind, I could hear the preacher saying, "If you don't accept Christ today, it's possible that you may not ever go to heaven." Somehow, I knew it was very important to get saved, so I stood up and went to the front of the church. The pastor asked us all to repeat after him, "Dear Lord Jesus. I am a sinner. I have done many wrong things. I ask you to forgive me and to come into my heart. Thank you that I am now a member of the Family of God and I can look forward to heaven. After I prayed that prayer, a cloud removed from over my head. I no longer felt depressed and alone. I felt that God was with me. And of course, it was wonderful when I could finally drink the grape juice and eat the crackers in the Lord's Supper.

Life Application: Recognize that you need to be involved with a church.

Drama: (Map of the world, act out which place that God prefers most):
Characters: God and you
You: You probably would prefer one of these places
God: No, I most love Jerusalem!

LESSON 5: Hiding or Kind of Lying

Draw a picture of the thing that you lied about or the place where you hid.

Picture E

Directions: Color in the dresses in the closet.

Lesson 5 – Amazing hides from the neighbors

Key Vocabulary

Column A	Column B/Synonyms	Column C/Antonyms
1. Identity	a. be invisible	a. sight
2. Disappear	b. no money	b. visible
3. Problem	c. a closed space	c. late
4. Ride n.	d. add to the family	d. open space
5. Prove	e. get out of sight	e. fortunately
6. Unfortunately	f. family name	f. orphan
7. Adopt	g. a sad thing	g. no name/bastard
8. hide	h. trouble	h. reject
9. Closet	i. drive	i. rich
10. Poor	j. to show truth	j. answer

Insert the right word from column A into a sentence below:

1. If you do not have parents, it is a joy to be _____ into a family .

2. Don't _____ if you have done something wrong.

3. Put your clothes in a _____ so your room can look neat.

4. Never take a _____ from a stranger.

5. If you have a _____ that you can't solve, ask for help.

6. No one is _____ who has a kind heart.

7. When she put on the cream, the sore _____.

8. Show your student _____ card if a teacher asks for it.

9. Always _____ you are an excellent student by being on time.

10. _____, only one person can be the winner!

Lesson 5

Comprehension Quiz/Discussion Questions

Directions: Students should copy the questions from below onto a sheet of paper and answer them in groups of two or by themselves. Then discuss as a large group.

1. What was Amazing's problem?
2. Where did her parents go?
3. What happened to her parents?
4. What kind of ride did they try to take?
5. Did Cinderella's father want to adopt Amazing?
6. Why couldn't he?
7. Where did Amazing go after her parents disappeared?
8. Why did Amazing hide in the closet?
9. If someone saw Amazing, what would happen?
10. Have you ever had to hide for any reason?

10. Group discussion.
9. She would have a problem over her identity
8. So no one would see her
7. She went to live with Cinderella and her family
6. His wife had died.
5. Yes
4. A boat ride
3. They disappeared
2. To the islands
1. She did not have an identity card

Dialogue- A Good Reason to Hide

Sir Milton: Come here, my girl.
Cinderella: Yes, papa!

Sir Milton: Sorry but, I have some bad news.
Cinderella: What is it, papa?

Sir Milton: Her parents' boat disappeared.
Cinderella: Oh, no! Poor Amazing!

Sir Milton: She doesn't have an id card, so she will have to hide from others or she will have to leave our home.

Cinderella: Okay, papa! If anyone comes to our cottage, I'll tell her to hide.

Discussion 5/Journal questions

Have you ever lied? What happened?

_____
_____
_____
_____
_____

Why doesn't God want us to lie?

_____
_____
_____
_____
_____

What does it mean that God is our Master?

_____
_____
_____
_____
_____

Sometimes, are you trying to be too nice to an adult or friend and doing the wrong thing?

_____
_____
_____
_____
_____

DEVOTION 5: Hiding/Lying But My Master Sees All

The reason why you don't need to lie

Lesson #5 – Hiding– Just like Amazing had to learn how to honor Cinderella and her family even though they were so different than her, so God wants us to learn how to be loyal to Him because He is our Lord and Master, Adonai. This does not mean that we are forced slaves. It means that we are in a relationship with a God who is looking at everything we do. Whereas teachers often only see what you do in class, and parents in the home, God is looking at everything! He is seeing what we do. He is looking at why we do it. For example, you may bring money to God to church because your parents told you to, then shove it into the offering basket. God is looking at why you shoved that money. Was it because you wanted to spend it on a few candy bars or save it up for yourself for later. He wants to be Lord of our lives. He wants us to love being an important part of His kingdom and to serve Him with seriousness.

Think about this Theme: There is a Kingdom Allegiance/Loyalty

1. Malachi 1:6 (The Lord is our master and expects to be honored) If I am your father and master, where are the honor and respect I deserve?

2. Matthew 6:33 (The Lord is our Master and expects to be first) But seek ye first the kingdom of God, and his righteousness; and all these things shall be added unto you.

3. Exodus 23:24-25 (The Lord is our Master that is why we cannot bow down to idols or pray to statues) You shall not worship their gods, nor serve them, nor do according to their deeds; but you shall utterly overthrow them...

4. Daniel 3:28 (If you tell others that Jesus is your Lord and Master, the Lord can use that to turn hearts to himself.) Then Nebuchadnezzar said, "Praise be to the God of Shadrach, Meshach and Abednego, who has sent his angel and rescued his servants! They trusted in him and defied the king's command and were willing to give up their lives rather than serve or worship any god except their own God.

We show respect for our King by obeying Him and pledging our allegiance to Him, even when it get's hard and we want to do the wrong thing. When we honor the Lord, the Lord will honor us but if we dishonor Him, we welcome problems into our lives.

Child Testimony

Once I became a Christian, I became an obedient child. I was always at school. Usually, I would go early. Then I would stay afterwards and play with my younger sister. I was always minding my teachers and obeying my leaders.

One day while I was at a friend's church, they asked all children age 10 years old and older to stand up. They showed us a picture of black female diva and asked us to come forward and bow down to her. I looked at my mom and asked her if I should stand up. She said, "Yes!" The speaker said we would be joining a special sorority that is like Girl Scouts, but it wasn't.

I always admired and wanted to be a girl scout, but my older sister whispered to me, "No, don't do it!". I stood up anyway and gave my allegiance to be involved in the special sisterhood. Later that day in our bedroom, my older sister told me, "You forgot what they taught us at Sunday School. Remember the pastor said, "We only bow down on our knees to Jesus!"

From that day onward some kind of feelings of sadness came into my life. I didn't understand until many years later that I had disobeyed God and His heart. All I had to do was ask God to forgive me, but I thought it didn't matter. How wrong I was! Later on, after I had asked Jesus Christ to forgive me, I found out that she was a female figure of a black God.

Drama: Four people bow and worship movie stars but one person says, "I cannot. I only worship Jesus Christ."

Life Application: Write down inside of your Bible, I will only worship the God of the Bible and bow down to Jesus Christ only.

LESSON 6: THE NOSY MAN

Draw a picture of someone who made you feel bad.

Lesson 6 – The Nosy Man

Key Vocabulary

Column A	Column B/Synonyms	Column C/Antonyms
1. Report	a. one person	a. nobody
2. Castle	b. saw	b. missed
3. Move	c. become larger	c. a promise
4. home	d. a written paper	d. close
5. anyone	e. met	e. shrink
6. Far	f. a king's house	f. someone
7. No one	g. wiggle	g. shack
8. noticed	h. distance	h. avoided
9. know	i. house of love	i. shelter
10. grew	j. not even one	j. shed

Insert the right word from column A into a sentence below:

1. If you do your homework, your parents will get a good _____.
2. The bump on her face _____ because she did not wash it.
3. _____ can make a sandwich but not cook a meal.
4. No one _____ the dust on the edge of the window.
5. I did not _____ he was a prince because he liked to fish.
6. _____ quickly if you have something to do.
7. The _____ was open to everyone to visit, not just the rich..
8. _____ is poor who has a good heart.
9. How _____ to the market?
10. There's no place like _____!

Lesson 6

Comprehension Quiz/Discussion Questions

Directions: Students should copy the questions from below onto a sheet of paper and answer them in groups of two or by themselves. Then discuss as a large group.

1. Why would Amazing have to go to the children's home?
2. Who could report her?
3. Who would the report be made to?
4. Was the children's home close to Cinderella's house?
5. Did anyone notice Amazing?
6. Did Amazing get adopted?
7. Did Amazing grow up?
8. Who was the closest person to Amazing?
9. How old was she?
10. How old are you?

1. She did not have any parents
2. Anyone
3. The king
4. no, it was far away
5. Noone
6. No
7. Yes (which tells us that we can have problems, but we don't have to stop growing)
8. Amazing and her father
9. It does not say. It implies that she became a young woman
10. Not old enough for marriage yet, right!

Dialogue-

Cinderella: Hello, Old man Jeeters.

Old Man Jeeters: How are you princess?

Cinderella: Fine and you?

Old Man Jeeters: I'm...what's that!

(he points at the house where there is a shadow)

Cinderella: Oh, that's nothing.

Old Man Jeeters: No, I heard something.

(he looks inside the window)

Cinderella: (covers the window with her body)
You're very funny Old Man Jeeters. I'm sure it's just the cat.

Discussion 6/ Journal Questions

Have you ever met a nosy person? Someone who likes to be in your business?

_____

_____

_____

_____

_____

What makes you feel uncomfortable or scared?

_____

_____

_____

_____

_____

Does God care if we sometimes get hurt? Or someone tries to harm us?

_____

_____

DEVOTION 6: The Nosy Man is not Bigger than El Elyon, The Most High God

How God protects us from someone who tries to hurt us

Lesson #6 - The Nosy Man – Just like Cinderella and Amazing were fearing the power that the other people had over them, so we should see that the Lord Most High is The Highest Power (El Elyon) ever! Sometimes, when we meet big people especially if you are of a short height and light weight, you can feel small. Then when you hear on the news that this big person did some unkind action which hurt someone else, you can feel so small. For example, there was a story in news about two men who stood in line to get into a popular movie. Somehow before the movie began, they got into an argument and one man (who was stronger than the other) picked up the smaller man up and threw him on the ground. It's easy to think that it could happen again, that someone who is stronger or older or wealthier could mess up your life, right? But the Bible teaches that no matter how big or strong people get down here. God is always the greater One. In fact in Genesis 14:19-20, "Blessed be Abraham of the Most High God, possessor of heaven and earth, and blessed be the Most High who has delivered your enemies into your hand." This means that there is no enemy so great which cannot be conquered by trusting in the Most High God.

Think about this Theme: There is a King who is Above all kings or The King of kings and Lord of lords

1. Isa. 45:5 (The Bible says there is only one true God) I am the LORD, and there is no other, besides me there is no God

2. Matthew 12:40 (Jesus is called greater than King Solomon) The Queen of the South … came from the ends of the earth to listen to Solomon's wisdom, and now something greater than Solomon is here.

3. 1 Timothy 6:14-15 (The Bible calls Jesus greater than all Superpowers) Lord Jesus Christ: Which in his times he shall show, who is the blessed and only Potentate (superpower), the King of kings, and Lord of lords. This means that no matter how powerful a country can become they will never be more powerful than the Lord God Himself.

4. 1 John 4:4 (The Bible says a greater one lives inside of us since the first day of our salvation) You, dear children, are from God and have overcome them, because the one who is in you is greater than the one who is in the world. There is no God like our God. There is no one like Him.

5. Proverbs 21:1 (The Bibles says that God will direct leaders to do what He wants) the king's heart is in the hand of the LORD, as the rivers of water: he turns it wheresoever he wills.

Child Testimony:

Child Testimony: Because I loved to pray, I prayed a lot. Sometimes, I saw God answer my prayers and sometimes, I did not. But when I was in sixth grade, God definitely protected me.

One of my mother's customers was a photographer who had a beautiful condo with a pool in a rich neighborhood. He told my mother that we could come to his house to swim. He was an old man and didn't have a wife or a family. For over one year, he would cook meals for us and give us money but he never did anything bad. Then one day while my brother and sisters were downstairs swimming, I was upstairs going into the bathroom. I went to close the bathroom door, but he put his feet inside of it and said, "Can I come in!"

Immediately, I knew something was wrong. I yelled, "No!!!! Lord Jesus help me!" Immediately, the man walked away. He said, "I wasn't going to do anything!." But I felt different. I never we to his home again! Later, after I became an adult, I realized that God heard and answered my prayers for protection that I would pray at the side of my bed every night. Though that was a big man, truly God was the greater One for me that day and turned the man's heart away from doing the wrong thing.

Drama: Rich and royal people (the Egyptians for example) decide to do starve their workers, but God sends food (birds and bread from heaven).

Life Application: Pray that if you see your teachers or parents doing something wrong, that God will change their minds. Pray if you ever have fear that someone will hurt you or your family.

LESSON 7: Strangely Odd

Draw a picture of someone or something that is strange to you.

Directions: Color in the horse and the carriage

Picture G

Lesson 7 – Strange People

Key Vocabulary

Column A	Column B/Synonyms	Column C/Antonyms
1. Expect	a. visitors	a. gave
2. Brought	b. took	b. normal
3. Strange	c. listened	c. oinking
4. Woman	d. a written paper	d. ignored
5. group	e. sounding like a horse	e. shrink
6. Cook	f. a king's house	f. raw
7. heard	g. annual	g. day
8. neighing	h. band	h. aliens
9. year	i. lady	i. only one
10. guests	j. odd	j. gentleman

Insert the right word from column A into a sentence below:

1. Teachers_____ all of us to act politely.

2. Most people have to _____their own food.

3. Friendly people always welcome new people to their _____.

4. The mother _____ the child to the crib.

5. If you frown all the time, people will think you're _____.

6. Horses _____ when they arrive at a new place.

7. A kind _____ like to help sick people.

8. Twelve months equal one _____.

9. I _____ you the first time you called me.

10. The _____ received a free coffee with their room.

Lesson 7
Comprehension Quiz/Discussion Questions

Directions: Students should copy the questions from below onto a sheet of paper and answer them in groups of two or by themselves. Then discuss as a large group.

1. Why would Amazing have to go to the children's home?
2. Who could report her?
3. Who would the report be made to?
4. Was the children's home close to Cinderella's house?
5. Did anyone notice Amazing?
6. Did Amazing get adopted?
7. Did Amazing grow up?
8. Who was the closest person to Amazing?
9. How old was she?
10. How old are you?

10. Not old enough for marriage yet, right!
9. It does not say. It implies that she became a young woman
8. Amazing and her father
7. Yes (which tells us that we can have problems, but we don't have to stop growing)
6. No
5. Noone
4. no, it was far away
3. The king
2. Anyone
1. She did not have any parents

Dialogue-

Wickedra: I've married a man who is very rich and we are going to be #1 in his house.

Nisty: Oh, I hope he has lots of steak and fancy cakes.

Illamannera: Yes, I can be the boss of the house.

Misbehavia: Well, if I can't be the boss, I'll just fight about it.

Wickedra: That's enough girls. Try to look normal even if you are a little strange.

Discussion 7/ Journal Questions

How should you treat someone who is mean to you?

_____

_____

Have you ever seen any adults make a mistake? Why do you suppose adults make mistakes?

_____

_____

What can you do if someone is mistreating you?

_____

_____

Who do you believe the most concerning your identity?

_____

_____

DEVOTION 7: Strangely Odd but not
Mistreating Anyone Because of the Lord's Holiness
How God wants you to deal with strange or mean people

Lesson #7 - Strangely Odd - Just like Cinderella realized that she should not mistreat her stepmother and stepsisters, so God doesn't want us to mistreat anyone. We may meet someone who acts impolite or weird, but we should ask The Holy One Jehovah Makkadesh to give us the ability to treat everyone well. The way we treat people shows what gym we are drawing our strength from. If we are treating people poorly, most likely we are not getting strength from God, we are getting it from our own abilities. Human strength is limited. Just like the flesh can only lift so much weight, so by our own charm we can only handle certain kinds of situations easily. Difficult people will challenge you to pray for them or hate them. God wants us to love, but this is only possible by His Strength, and He is the Holy One, Jehovah Makkadesh.

Theme: There is a kingdom code of conduct which is love and other behaviors which means we need to Be loving when we don't want to be.

Jn. 13:35 (God asks us to be careful about the way we treat others.) By this shall all men know that ye are my disciples, if ye have love one to another.

Galatians 5:22 (God asks us to be full of good qualities.) But the fruit of the Spirit is love, joy, peace, patience, kindness, goodness, faithfulness, gentleness, self-control;

1 Jn 4:7-8 (God asks us to be known as loving people) Beloved, let us love one another, for love is from God; and everyone who loves is born of God and knows God. The one who does not love.

Ephesians 4:32 (God asks us to stop all bad behavior and to forgive others quickly) Get rid of all bitterness, rage and anger, outcry and slander, along with every form of malice. Be kind and tender-hearted to one another, forgiving each other just as in Christ God forgave you.

Psalm 34:13 (God asks us to be honest.) Keep thy tongue from evil, and thy lips from speaking lies.

Matthew 5: 35 (God asks us to not use profanity or bad words) But I tell you not to swear at all: either by heaven, for it is God's throne; or by the earth, for it is His footstool; or by Jerusalem, for it is the city of the great King.

Child Testimony

Child Testimony: Friendships were always my favorite toy. I never cared if I had dolls to play with, or mud pies or a game. I just liked being with my friends. I had a very dear friend from school whose name was Stephanie. Every day at recess, she and I would play together and then get into line. One day, I invited her to our home. At that time, some of my mom's friends were staying with us. To my surprise, my mom's friend's daughter knew Stephanie. They told me that they had grown up together and gone to preschool together since they were 3 years old. They had not seen each other in a while but they were still best friends. I was not. I was so hurt, that I ran into my room crying. I didn't understand why the girls were so mean. My mom came into my room and told me, "Remember Jesus is the best friend and no one can take Him away from you. Also, you can play with your sisters." Two weeks later, Stephanie came over again. She and Geneva said, "You're out! We're best friends and you are not. I had a doll and a book in my hand. This time, it did not hurt me. "I said, "It's okay, I have my sisters and plenty of other things to do. You two enjoy!" They were shocked and could not believe that they couldn't get me to cry. I was getting closer and closer to Jesus and learning to make friends with many other students from my class and just enjoy my family.

Drama: Act like someone just stole your lunch. Tell them, good words instead of bad like, "whoever took my lunch box must have been very hungry. May God bless them with abundant food."

Life Application: Say, I will use good words not bad words

LESSON 8: Lost as cats

Draw a picture of a place where you got lost.

Picture H

Directions: Color in Cinderella's hair and dress.

Lesson 8 – Lost

Key Vocabulary

Column A	Column B/Synonyms	Column C/Antonyms
1. Door	a. wed	a. frown
2. Wife	b. female child	b. husband
3. daughter	c. crazy	c. dog
4. bench	d. entrance	d. ground
5. Cat	e. believe	e. immediately
6. marry	f. after a long while	f. divorce
7. hope	g. seat	g. son
8. wild	h. furry animal	h. can't trust
9. smile	i. mate	i. calm
10. finally	j. grin	j. wall

Insert the right word from column A into a sentence below:

1. After leaving the _____, he walked the dog.

2. My _____ is the exact image of my wife.

3. The _____ chased the dog around the room.

4. Your _____ makes people like you more.

5. Always lock the _____ after entering.

2. _____, I passed my test.

6. Choose a _____ who loves you more than your money.

7. If a _____ meows, give it some milk.

8. No matter what happens, there is always _____.

9. Wait until you're older to _____?

10. Did you know you sleep like a _____ bull?

Dialogue- Help Needed!

Wickedra: Excuse me, sir. Can you help us!

Sir Milton: Ah, yes, my lady. What can I do for you?

Wickedra: Do you have a fine house?

Sir Milton: What's that? I suppose you could say a man's home *is* his castle.

Wickedra: Oh good, then perhaps my three daughters and I can come to work for you as your maids. They have just lost their father.

Sir Milton thought a minute: Well, believe it or not, I don't need a maid, but I do need a wife.

Wickedra screams to her daughters: We're rich!

Lesson 8

Comprehension Quiz/Discussion Questions

Directions: Students should copy the questions from below onto a sheet of paper and answer them in groups of two or by themselves. Then discuss as a large group.

1. What kind of relationship did Cinderella and her father have?
2. Where did Cinderella's father meet Wickedra?
3. What word does Wickedra remind you of?
4. How about Nisty, Illamannera and Misbehavia?
5. Why were the women in the town square?
6. How did Sir Milton say they looked?
7. Why did Wickedra have a wild smile?
8. Did Sir Milton marry Wickedra?
9. Why did Sir Milton marry Wickedra?
10. Where was Amazing hiding?

10. In the closet!
9. He needed a wife
8. yes
7. She was embarrassed.
6. Like lost cats
5. They were looking for work.
4. Nasty, Ill-mannered, Misbehavior
3. Wicked
2. Distressia
1. Loving

Discussion 8/Journal Questions

Have you ever felt like a lost cat?

_____

_____

What do you do when you feel lost?

_____

_____

Was anyone in the Bible ever lost? Who was it and how were they found?

_____

_____

DEVOTION 8: Lost but The Holy Spirit is My Guide

Why you're never truly lost with God

Lesson #8 - Lost – Just like Amazing's parents got lost at sea, sometimes, we too get lost and need the Good Shepherd to lead us to safety. Sometimes, we travel down a street and don't know how to get home or sometimes we simply do not know what to do. If you have asked Jesus Christ into your heart, He will give you the Holy Spirit to lead and guide you all of the days of your life. All you have to do is say, "Lord, show me what to do and where to go".

Think about this Theme: <u>There is a Kingdom Guide</u> who is the Holy Spirit

1. John 16:7 (The Bible tells us that after Jesus left, another representative from Heaven came here to help us who is the Holy Spirit.) Nevertheless I tell you the truth; **It is expedient** for you **that I go away**: for if I go not away, the Comforter will not come unto you; but if I depart, I will send him unto you... Jesus wasn't the only one who came from heaven to help us. The Holy Spirit also came.

2. Matthew 16:13 (The Holy Spirit is now our guide to keep us on the right track and from messing up our lives.) However when He, the Spirit of Truth, is come, He will guide you into all truth; for He shall not speak from Himself, but whatsoever He shall hear, that shall He speak; and He will show you things to come. In other words, you don't have to have all of the answers to your problems, God can solve them for you.

3. Mark 16:19-20 (Read carefully that after Jesus left, the Holy Spirit was working with the disciples) Then the Master Jesus, after briefing them, was taken up to heaven, and he sat down beside God in the place of honor. And the disciples went everywhere preaching, the Master working right with them, validating the Message with indisputable evidence.]

4. Act16:6 (Sometimes the Holy Spirit will forbid you to do something, especially when you are a child and not an adult yet. You may find that your parents say "No" because they do not believe an activity is healthy or safe for you. Listen to them!) **6** Paul and his companions traveled throughout the region of Phrygia and Galatia, having been kept by the Holy Spirit from preaching the word in the province of Asia.

Child Testimony:

One day it was early in the morning and I had turned 13 years of age. At this age, you could get a job with the community day care center at the park. It was about 6:45 am. on a summer morning. I had to be at work at 7:30 am. because I was getting paid to take care of five-year-olds. I was wearing shorts and gym shoes.

I left my house while most of my family members were still sleeping. I walked south on my street then turned right. I was walking as quickly as I could to make my bus at 7:00 a.m. All of a sudden, a man came out of a house about three doors down from me. He was wearing a long black leather jacket and walking quickly in front of me. He seemed strange.

As I got closer to him, I could see that he was trying to look out of the corner of his eyes without turning around. As I was about to pass him, I heard a voice inside of me say, "Move". I moved to the right of the man just as he turned to my side and violently punched the air. I sprinted to my bus and it arrived right on time, so that even if the man had wanted to take it, he couldn't. I don't know what the man had in his hand, but if I had not moved when that little voice inside of me told me to do so, I probably would have been knocked out. I think he was drunk or something.

Drama: Two friends invite you for ice cream but you say, "I must pray first. Go to your room and say this prayer "Dear father, Lead and guide me by your Holy Spirit" and come back say, "So sorry, but I can't go this time."

Life Application: Pray about where you go before you go. Use the prayer above.

LESSON 9: Learning how to Share

Draw a picture of something you shared with a brother or sister or friend.

Directions: Color in Amazing's outfit and the carpet and wall behind them.

Lesson 9 – Learning How to Share or Help Others

Key Vocabulary

Column A	Column B/Synonyms	Column C/Antonyms
1. Wicked	a. unpleasant	a. polite
2. Nasty	b. exhausted	b. none
3. illmannered	c. to say yes	c. hard
4. misbehave	d. without trying	d. ground
5. sour	e. cruel	e. good
6. nice	f. all	f. pleasant
7. tired	g. kind	g. son
8. easy	h. ugly	h. mean
9. Entire	i. rude	i. calm
10. agree	j. nato act naughty	j. disagree

Insert the right word from column A into a sentence below:

1. Let's try to _____ on which one to buy.

2. Children who love to _____ get into a lot of trouble.

3. Don't be _____ because someone stepped on your foot.

4. Your _____ ways are like a witch.

5. Your _____ family is cool.

2. Some old people are _____ because they are tired.

6. Helping someone is _____ if you're a nice person.

7. Exercise regularly or you will be _____ all of the time.

8. No matter what happens, there is always _____.

9. Because she was _____, she ate more than her guests.

10. Was the wolf _____ to the three little pigs?

Dialogue- Cinderella gets an A for sharing

Cinderella: This is my room.

Nisty: Wow, it's pretty! I wish it were...

Illamannera: ...Ours! (grabbing pillows)

Misbehavia: It is ours. This whole house is ...

Wickedra: Girls, what are you doing up there? Come down at once.

Sir Milton: Yes, it's time for supper.

Cinderella: Oh, you girls are so funny.

Nisty, whispering: That wasn't a joke.

Illamannera, whispering: She's serious.

Misbehavia, whispering: We'll be back. So do get too comfortable in there.

Sir Milton (turning to the girls): What are you girls whispering about over there.

Cinderella: It's nothing that I can't handle, Dad!

Sir Milton (Smiling): You're right! I have the most wonderful daughter...
Wickedra:...daughters!

Lesson #9

Comprehension Quiz/Discussion Questions

Directions: Students should copy the questions from below onto a sheet of paper and answer them in groups of two or by themselves. Then discuss as a large group.

1. Why did the houseguests try to be nice?
2. What did Wickedra tell Cinderella she would have to do?
3. Why did Cinderella's father leave?
4. How long was he going to be gone?
5. Where did Wickedra meet up with Cinderella?
6. What kind of housework does Cinderella have to do?
7. Does Cinderella seem afraid of her new mother?
8. Does the new mother appear to like Cinderella?
9. Why did Cinderella want Wickedra and her daughters to leave?
10. Why did the four ladies agree to leave the house?

1. Because Cinderella's father was around
2. All of the housework
3. To get Amazing adopted/to discover Amazin'g identity
4. Not sure, it doe not say
5. Kitchen
6. Dusty, dirty work
7. Not really. She is rather confident.
8. Not really
9. So she could have time with Amazing out of the closet
10. Because they wanted Cinderella to serve them and they wanted to shop.

Discussion 9/ Journal Questions

Do you see your family as poor or rich or...?

_____

_____

What do you do when you don't have enough money, but really want to buy something?

_____

_____

Have you started to tithe yet? Why is tithing so important?

_____

_____

_____

_____

_____

DEVOTION 9: Sharing Because the Lord Can Provide More When I Run Out

Why God shares with us

Lesson #9 - Sharing – Just like Cinderella learned to share her time with her new family members, so the Lord wants us to learn the share because He is our Provider (Jireh). God never runs out of anything….Money, time, strength, grace! He's got it all. But as humans we often run low like cars needing gas. We tend to have to go to the gas station to refuel a lot. But Luke 6:38 says, "Give and you will receive". This means that we should not be afraid to be a blessing, because God will bless us back.

Theme: <u>There is Kingdom Money.</u>

1. Philippians 4:19-20 (If you are a member of God's family, you can trust God to provide for you) And my God will supply every need of yours according to his riches in glory in Christ Jesus. To God and our Father be glory forever and ever.

2. Malachi 3:10 (If you give to God your tithes and offerings, God gives to you more) Bring ye all the tithes into the storehouse, that there may be meat in mine house, and prove me now herewith, saith the LORD of hosts, if I will not open you the windows of heaven...

3. Matthew 17:25-27 (If your family needs immediate money, you can ask God to do a miracle for you!) When Peter came into the house, Jesus was the first to speak. "What do you think, Simon?" he asked. "From whom do the kings of the earth collect duty and taxes—from their own children or from others?" "From others," Peter answered. "Then the children are exempt," Jesus said to him. "But so that we may not cause offense, go to the lake and throw out your line. Take the first fish you catch; open its mouth and you will find a four-drachma coin. Take it and give it to them for my tax and yours."

4. Matthew 25:24-27 (If you choose to not give to the church, God will not like it) He also who had received the one talent came forward, saying, 'Master, I knew you to be a hard man, reaping where you did not sow, and gathering where you scattered no seed, so I was afraid, and I went and hid your talent in the ground. But his master answered him, 'You wicked and slothful servant! You knew that I reap where I have not sown and gather where I scattered no seed? Then you ought to have invested my money with the bankers, and at my coming I should have received what was my own with interest. So take the talent from him and give it to him who has the ten talents.

Child Testimony:

Child Testimony: When I was growing up, my parents were always struggling with money. My mom used to stand in the living room window looking out and saying, "I don't know how we are going to make it." I also used to stand in the window with her and praying for our family. But I knew that we were not giving God 10% of our income. When the basket was passed around, mom usually dug into the bottom of her purse and gave whatever coins she found in there. If the pastor asked us to bring an offering to the front of the church, mom usually dug around in her purse and gave each one of us a coin. Therefore, when I became an adult, I also gave God whatever I wanted to. I felt that I was doing better than my mom because I usually gave dollars. But I knew that I was supposed to give 10% so I was disobeying God. Finally, after I graduated from college, I made a commitment to always give my 10%. I found that I never had problems with money after that. Even my college debts of thousands of dollars were paid off within one year.

DRAMA: family needs 3000 for rent. The father doesn't want to pay tithes, but gives 300 to the church for the tithes in and all the money for rent is poured out on them.

Life Application: Be a tither.

LESSON #10: Do You like Yourself

Draw a picture of yourself. Tell a friend what you like the most about yourself.

Picture J

Directions: Color Amazing and her parents' sweaters and make their bottoms black.

Lesson 10 – Do you like yourself

Key Vocabulary

Column A	Column B/Synonyms	Column C/Antonyms
1. Disappeared	a. child without parents	a. polite
2. Proved	b. surely	b. to say but not show
3. papers	c. to provide **evidence**	c. fake documents
4. real	d. issue	d. hag
5. identity	e. true	e. appeared
6. beggar	f. young lady of worth	f. rich person
7. orphan	g. poor person	g. definitely not
8. Of course	h. legal documents	h. heir
9. princess	i. family name	i. anonymous
10. problem	j. vanished	j. fake

Insert the right word from column A into a sentence below:

1. Once her parents died, she had to go to the home for _____.

2. He was forgiven, so his bad record _____.

3. If you don't have _____ you may have to leave the country.

4. _____ every human has a mother and father.

5. If you did not cheat, _____ it!

2. All girls can be a _____ if they believe.

6. Helping someone is _____ if you're a nice person.

7. Unfortunately, _____ only receive a few nickels and dimes.

8. Please stop! What is your _____?

9. Your _____ is more than your first and last name.

10. Love is _____. You can feel it.

Dialogue- Amazing doesn't understand kindness

Sir Milton: Where's Amazing?
Cinderella: In our room, dad.

Sir Milton: Why didn't come down for dinner?
Cinderella: I think she's a little shy.

(suddenly Amazing appears)

Sir Milton: Good evening, Amazing.
Cinderella: yes, so glad you could join us!

Amazing: Thank you
Sir Milton: Why are you standing over there? Please have a seat.

Amazing: I don't want to give you any trouble. You just go ahead to eat and I'll watch you.

Sir Milton: Nonsense! You'll dine at table just like Cinderella and myself. (Sir Milton grabs the fork.) Beef or Chicken?

Lesson 10

Comprehension Quiz/Discussion Questions

Directions: Students should copy the questions from below onto a sheet of paper and answer them in groups of two or by themselves. Then discuss as a large group.

1. Did Amazing understand her identity?

2. What happened to her parents?

3. Where were her parents?

4. Were there many people from Amazing's country in the area?

5. Did Amazing think she was special?

6. How was Cinderella doing?

7. What did Sir Milton say to Amazing when she doubted her identity?

8. What did Amazing do when she came down for dinner?

9. Why was Amazing sad?

10. Why did Sir Milton say "nonsense"?

1. No. She wasn't sure who she was.
2. They disappeared on their boat ride.
3. Jamaican islands
4. No, because she was from China
5. She wasn't sure what to think about who she was.
6. Dusty, dirty work
7. She was encouraging.
8. Of course, you're a princess!
9. She stood and watched them eat.
10. Because he wanted Amazing to stop acting like a beggar.

Discussion 10/Journal Questions

What is a big family problem to you?

_____

Have you ever felt like you did not know who you are?

_____

What is your identity?

_____

What do you think about your value?

_____

Do you think some people are better than you?

_____

What proof do you have of your identity?

_____

_____

_____

DEVOTION 10: Liking Yourself Because You Are Made by The Creator

You should like yourself because you are made in God's image

Lesson #10 - Just like Amazing had to learn to accept her weaknesses so we have to learn to appreciate ourselves as the persons who The Creator made.
Do you like yourself just as you are? The Creator (Yahweh) likes you and made you special.

Think about the Theme: <u>In the Kingdom of God, Royalty is based on acceptance through Jesus Christ, not looks.</u>

1. Psalm 139: 14 (You may think that something went wrong in your body or looks but the Bible says you're wonderful just as you are!) I praise you because I am fearfully and wonderfully made; your works are wonderful, I know that full well.

2. Samuel 16:7 (You may think that God cares about whether you are beautiful or handsome or rich or poor, tall or short or have scars or blemishes, but He doesn't) But the LORD said to Samuel, "Do not look at his appearance or at his ... as man sees; for **man looks at the outward appearance**, but the Lord looks at the heart.

3. Matthew 6:31 (You may think that God's kingdom is all about eating the best or wearing the best but it isn't.) "Do **not** worry then, saying, 'What will **we** eat?' **or** 'What** will **we** drink?' **or** about your **body**, what **you will wear.**

4. Ephesians 1:3-6 (God cares about accepting you as you are in Jesus Christ, not about your own good things) Blessed *be* the God and Father of our Lord Jesus Christ, who has blessed us with every spiritual blessing in the heavenly *places* in Christ, just as He chose us in Him before the foundation of the world, that we should be holy and without blame before Him in love, having predestined us to adoption as sons by Jesus Christ to Himself, according to the good pleasure of His will, to the praise of the glory of His grace, by which He made us accepted in the Beloved.

God created everyone unique and special.

Child Testimony:

I was born blind, but I should have been seeing. There was an accident at the hospital in which the doctors had placed too much iodine in my eyes resulting in weak veins. They sent me home with my mom and dad and informed them that they could sue the hospital if they wanted to. But being a Baptist, my mom said, "No, we are going to pray!" Everyday she prayed over my eyes and one day when she looked at me, she noticed that my eyes followed her around the room. I was about 6 months old. She took me back to the hospital and the doctors said, "Yes, indeed! She can see!" It was the biggest miracle my mother and I had ever experienced.

Life Application: Write a note to another Christian who made you angry and tell them you accept them because of Christ, not because of their behavior.

DRAMA: The sweetest girl is always at the front then a student wearing a monster mask is asked by the teacher to lead the line but the sweet girl says, "no fair. He is bad". But the teacher says, "We treat everyone special here."

LESSON 11 My Bad Thing

Draw a picture of your bad thing. Discuss this with your teacher in private one at a time.

Picture K

Directions: Color us in! Use a thin red marker for the rose.

Lesson 11 – Your Bad thing

Key Vocabulary

Column A	Column B/Synonyms	Column C/Antonyms
1. promise	a. breath hard	a. normal
2. turn	b. party	b. die
3. ball	c. occur	c. fake documents
4. reply	d. wish	d. hag
5. hope	e. bang	e. tap
6. happen	f. assure	f. give up
7. finish	g. change age	g. blow
8. knock	h. prepare	h. lie
9. push	i. odd	i. remain silent
10. huff	j. say	j. cease

Insert the right word from column A into a sentence below:

1. The runner was so fast that she was _____.

2. High school students go to a party like a _____.

3. Please _____before entering a bathroom.

4. If you don't_____ your food you may not get dessert.

5. Did you_____ to his letter?

6. _____ the shopping cart to the rack, please.

7. Good things _____ when you are happy.

8. When will you _____ 18?

9. Don't make a _____ that you can't keep.

10. The only person without _____ is a dead man.

Lesson 11

Comprehension Quiz/Discussion Questions

Directions: Students should copy the questions from below onto a sheet of paper and answer them in groups of two or by themselves. Then discuss as a large group.

1. Did Sir Milton know Amazing's parents?

2. Did Amazing's parents have a special dream for her?

3. Amazing wanted what kind of things to happen to her?

4. Did Cinderella give Amazing some advice?

5. What was it?

6. Who knocked on the door?

7. What did Illamannera hear?

8. What did Misbehavia do?

9. Did she hurt herself?

10. Were the three girls nice?

10. Not really
9. No. It seems like she is used to doing this.
8. Pushed the door open with her shoulder!
7. She demanded entrance.
6. Nisty
5. Believe. Stay positive
4. Yes
3. Good things
2. Yes, to go to the ball
1. Yes.

Dialogue

Amazing: That bird is so funny.

Cinderella: Yes, that's why his name is funny bone.

Amazing: that's better than chicken bone

Cinderella: Yes, or wish bone.

Bird: Gawk, or broken bone!

Discussion 11/Journal Questions

What is your parents' dream for you?

_____

_____

What is your dream for yourself?

_____

_____

Is it the same thing?

_____

_____

DEVOTION 11: My Bad Thing Can Turn to Good As I Look To The Almighty

What can God do with your bad thing?

Lesson #11 – My Bad Thing – Just like Amazing had to learn to turn away from her anger, so The Lord wants us to turn away from our weaknesses through His power because He is El Shaddai , The Almighty, Excellent One. You can never do something so bad that God cannot forgive you. Not only will He forgive you, but He will also give you the ability to correct your actions. Nevertheless, because God does everything well, He wants to get us to the point where we are not always messing up, but learning to do things the right way. We can do things the right way through The Almighty, El Shaddai.

Think about this Theme: <u>There is a Kingdom behavior of perfection</u>. This means that we should look for the best in every situation.

1. Matthew 5:48 (We should follow God's example of excellence in all things.) Be ye therefore perfect, even as your Father which is in heaven is perfect.

2. Genesis 17:1 (We should follow God's example of excellence and remember the one who walks through life with us always) When Abram was ninety-nine years old, the LORD appeared to him and said, "I am God Almighty; walk before me faithfully and be blameless.

3. 12 Corinthians 6:14-20 (We should follow God's example of excellence in not hanging out with people who do dirty things), "Come out from them and be separate, says the Lord. Touch no unclean thing, and I will receive you."[d]And, "I will be a Father to you, and you will be my sons and daughters, says the Lord Almighty."

Child Testimony:

Child Testimony: Once I had accepted Jesus Christ in my heart and was made a member of the church who could partake in the Lord's Supper. We were told that before we eat that, we must always ask God to forgive us and cleanse us if we ever did anything bad otherwise, when we ate the Lord's Supper, we could be sick. I took that seriously. Whereas before, I used to do whatever I wanted only fearing a spanking, I started to want to please God. Therefore, when my sisters said, "lets go pick the forbidden berries which my uncle had told us not to pick I said no. So they picked the berries anyway and gave me some to eat after they had returned. But when my uncle came home, at dinner time, he noticed the stains on their clothes and on their hands and asked them if they had been picking berries. They didn't say anything. Finally I spoke up and said theat they had picked them but I had not wanted to pick them. In the end they were puished but I was not. This experience taught me that it was important to do the right thing.

Because God is perfect, he has the power to help us to become the kind of people whom he delights in.

DRAMA – TOUCH NO UNCLEAN THING – Let's see what game can I play together – Write the following on the board. Find a volunteer who will talk through why they won't choose the negative ones.

Closet – Alone with a boy or a girl	Telephone – Calling people and pretending they won a prize	Pornography
Beating someone up today	Smoking	Monopoly
Bingo	Volleyball	Basketball

Life Application: I don't allow myself to say it's okay to do the wrong things. But if I do make a mistake I believe that God is strong enough to correct it for me.

LESSON 12 Cinderella's courage

Draw a picture of something that that you want but cannot have at this time.

Directions: Color the circles the colors or the rainbow

Picture L

Lesson 12 – Cinderella's Courage

Key Vocabulary

Column A	Column B/Synonyms	Column C/Antonyms
1. town	a. shine	a. before
2. Do my best (verb phrase)	b. blessing	b. Good!
3. beautiful	c. Try hard	c. bored
4. excited	d. rained	d. country
5. Sparkle	e. What a pity!	e. Give up!
6. after	f. private business	f. dried up
7. Sorry!	g. ready	g. ugly
8. Good luck	h. lovely	h. darken
9. Secret	i. city	i. public news
10. poured	j. later	j. curse

Insert the right word from column A into a sentence below:

1. _____ you go to the store, bring back my change.

2. Every bride is _____.

3. Please _____ me a drink of lemonade.

4. Don't say _____ if you don't mean it.

5. I get _____ when the phone rings.

6. This _____ does not have a fire department.

7. Not everyone has _____ on a test.

8. Sometimes, _____ stop us from getting help.

9. Always try to _____.

10. Happiness makes your eyes _____.

Lesson 12

Comprehension Quiz/Discussion Questions

Directions: Students should copy the questions from below onto a sheet of paper and answer them in groups of two or by themselves. Then discuss as a large group.

1. How many girls knew about the ball?
2. They were trying to look as beautiful as what insect?
3. Was it easy for Cinderella to make them beautiful ?
4. Did Cinderella have hopes of going to the ball?
5. What did Misbehavia do to Cinderella's dress?
6. What did Nisty say to her?
7. Did Cinderella cry because she couldn't go to the ball?
8. Who helped Cinderella get ready for the ball?
9. Did Cinderella and Amazing have a bet about the ball?
10. Who helped Amazing get to the ball?

10. No one
9. Yes, they had a coin toss.
8. Her fairy godmother
7. No, she believed good things would happen if she was good to others
6. Sorry you can't go to the ball
5. Poured plant water on it
4. Yes
3. No! It was hard work.
2. Butterflies
1. Everyone.

Dialogue- A long time ago!

Amazing: Oh no, what happened to your dress?

Cinderella: Misbehavia poured plant water over it.

Amazing: Oh, that girl!!! I wish I could...

Cinderella: Oh, don't say it.

Amazing: I know, I know, but... I won't.

Cinderella: Of course you won't. You've changed, but you used to be like that.

Amazing: Yes, once upon a time, a long, long time ago...

Discussion 12/Journal Questions

Have you ever wanted to give up?

_____

_____

_____

_____

Have you ever wanted to stop playing because you did not play well or people teased you?

_____

_____

_____

Have you ever wanted to stop praying?

_____

_____

_____

How can you keep going when you want to give up?

_____

DEVOTION 12: Never Giving Up on The Everlasting God

Why we never give up hope

Lesson #12 – Cinderella's Courage/Bravery/Endurance – Just like Cinderella was brave and never gave up on her dreams, so we should have faith and never give up on The Everlasting God (El Olam).

Think on this Theme: <u>There is a Kingdom Attitude which is Faith</u>, Endurance and Persistence

1. Isaiah 40:28 – (God never gets too tired for anything! He never gets worn out!) Do you not know? Have you not heard? The LORD is the everlasting God, the Creator of the ends of the earth. He will not grow tired or weary, and his understanding no one can fathom.

2. Matthew 9:28-30 – (Jesus asks us to believe in Him even when circumstances are unpleasant and hard) When he had gone indoors, the blind men came to him, and he asked them, "Do you believe that I am able to do this?" "Yes, Lord," they replied. Then he touched their eyes and said, "According to your faith let it be done to you"; and their sight was restored.

3. Matthew 7:7 (Persistence is Important because it will definitely be rewarded one day) Ask *and* keep on asking and it will be given to you; seek *and* keep on seeking and you will find; knock *and* keep on knocking and the door will be opened to you. Life is a marathon, not a sprint.

4. Revelation 2:10 (Be willing to trust God even until the day you die) Do not be afraid of what you are about to suffer. I tell you, the devil will put some of you in prison to test you, and you will suffer persecution for ten days. Be faithful, even to the point of death, and I will give you life as your victor's crown.

5. Psalm 16:8 (God can keep you consistent as you trust him to help you) I keep my eyes always on the LORD. With him at my right hand, I will not be shaken.

Child Testimony:

I come from a long line of great athletes. My dad and his brothers were all tall, over six feet and basketball champions. So in order to give us something to do after school, my mom put us in track and field. I did not know what it was, but I was willing to give it a try.

As things turned out. I was a horrible runner. The starter would shoot the gun, the runners would take off down the track and I was always the last person to cross the finish line. As expected, I often cried. But I still came to the track practice every day.

One day, we were at a track race and my coach said, "I know this is strange, but today I am going to have you run the race that is two times around the track." I ran it and I won it. After the race, my coach came up to me and said, "Do you know that was the race for all the girls age 10 to 11 in the city. This means your are the city champion. Next week, we will have the state championships. " I ran in that race too and I won it. Through this experience, I learned to have faith. Never give up because something is hard or impossible because things can become very good overnight.

DRAMA: Ask and keep on asking (One person acts like God and has money. The other is kneeling on a chair and asking for money. At first they ask for $100 and only get $5. But as they keep on asking they get more and more until they get the whole $100.)

Life Application: Don't be jealous when you see your friend's family get a new car etc. just think one day God will do a miracle for you too!

LESSON #13: Fears Away!

Draw a picture of something that you fear.

Picture M

Directions: Color Cinderella's dress light blue and her gloves white. Color the prince's jacket red.

Picture N

Directions: Color Amazing's dress green and the sky
blue.

Lesson 13 – Fears Away!

Key Vocabulary

Column A	Column B/Synonyms	Column C/Antonyms
1. Bow down	a. reaches	a. forehead
2. Brave	b. Look alive!	b. hate
3. belong	c. trailed	c. at ease
4. mind	d. pardoned	d. stand up
5. feelings	e. Delight	e. Give up!
6. enjoy	f. be a member	f. outsider
7. attention	g. emotions	g. stone
8. strikes	h. brain	h. stayed
9. followed	i. confident	i. remained
10. excused	j. lower	j. cowardly

Insert the right word from column A into a sentence below:

1. _____ every moment of your life if you can.
2. The prince _____ himself and rode toward the castle.
3. You _____ where people love and care for you.
4. Often control _____ of sadness or anger.
5. When you have a bully, always be _____ and smart.
6. In the presence of royalty, you should _____.
7. Be home before the clock _____ 6 p.m.
8. The sargent yelled to his privates, "_____!"
9. The son _____ whatever good thing he saw his parents do.
10. Keep your _____ free from garbage.

Lesson 13

Directions: Students should copy the questions from below onto a sheet of paper and answer them in groups of two or by themselves. Then discuss as a large group.

1. Who was the prince talking to at the ball?

2. Why did Cinderella look amazed?

3. Why did the guys look clean and brave?

4. Who was invited to the ball?

5. Why did Amazing feel embarrassed?

6. Why did she decide to stay at the ball?

7. Did anyone ask Amazing to dance?

8. Who ?

9. How many guys did Amazing dance with at the ball?

10. Who helped Amazing get to the ball?

1. Everyone.
2. Butterflies
3. No! It was hard work.
4. Yes
5. Poured plant water on it
6. Sorry you can't go to the ball
7. No, she believed good things would happen if she was good to others
8. Her fairy godmother
9. Yes, they had a coin toss.
10. Noone

Discussion 13/ Journal Questions

Have you ever felt fear? Why? What makes you fear?

_____

_____

_____

_____

Where do you feel you belong the most?

_____

_____

_____

_____

Where do you feel the most accepted and loved?

_____

_____

_____

_____

DEVOTION 13: Chase Fears Away
with The Lord is Peace, Jehovah Shalom
How to handle fears

Lesson #13 – Fears Away – Just like Amazing had to learn to be peaceful with Misbehavia, so we have to learn to be peaceful at all times because The Lord is Our Peace (Shalom). Yes, there may be event that occur in life to ruffle your feathers like a chicken, but hold tight light an eagle. Always be willing to give God a chance to show up and help you and your family and friends in any situation. God never wants any of us to feel like we have to suffer a bad situation in misery with no way out but PAIN. He can help us to find peace right in the middle of any situation that is too hard for us. In fact, He expects us to ALWAYS have peace in our hearts.

Think about this Theme: <u>The Kingdom Lifestyle is always peaceful</u>

We know that God wants us to be peaceful people because Jesus, Our Best Role Model was peaceful on the earth.

1. Isaiah 9:6 – (Jesus is the Prince of Peace) For to us a child is born, to us a son is given, and the government will be on his shoulders. And he will be called Wonderful Counselor, Mighty God, Everlasting Father, Prince of Peace.

2. John 14:27 – (Jesus wants us to have a Heart of Peace) **Peace I leave with you; my** peace I give to you. Not as the world gives do I give to you. Let not your hearts be troubled, neither let them be afraid.

3. Mark 4:39 – (Jesus role-modeled a Word of Peace) When **Jesus** woke up, he **rebuked the wind** and said to the waves, "Silence! Be still ... When the wind died down and it was completely calm. This means we can create peace by our words and actions.

Child Testimony:

One day when I was only 5 years old, my family and I were on a holiday trip. We were traveling in the mountains and had come up a very high ascent. Just when we were about to turn a very narrow curve, a huge truck came around the corner at the same time. Our car began to careen out of control.

My older sister who was only seven at that time screamed, "Jesus!" Immediately, my mom said a strong and took hold of the car and moved us to the side of the road safely. There was a moment of peace and joy that followed because of the miracle that occurred.

Over the years we were all puzzled because we could not explain to others how we had gotten to safety that day because the side of the road was across the street which was in front of the truck. It was a miracle and God had definitely brought us home peacefully that day!

LIFE APPLICATION: Decide who should be your friend and who should not be a close friend. When someone comes into your life who is not peaceful, pray about that person. The opposite of peace is trouble. Sometimes, we meet people who are troublemakers. These people are always at the principal's office for not listening to the teacher or mistreating the substitute. Watch who comes into your life and choose peaceful friends.

Drama: Give out labels, peaceful, nice, kind, smart, fighter, angry, easily offended, using bad words. Have students sit at a baseball game acting out their label.
Then one student should walk up and give the friend paper to anyone who is peaceful.

LESSON 14 – Adopted At last or/ Receiving Your Wish

Draw a picture of something you wish for or hope will happen.

Picture O

Directions: Color Amazing's dress and the walls

Lesson 14 – Adopted/ Getting your wish

Key Vocabulary

Column A	Column B/Synonyms	Column C/Antonyms
1. Bow down	a. reaches	a. forehead
2. Brave	b. Look alive!	b. hate
3. belong	c. trailed	c. at ease
4. mind	d. pardoned	d. stand up
5. feelings	e. Delight	e. Give up!
6. enjoy	f. be a member	f. outsider
7. attention	g. emotions	g. stone
8. strikes	h. brain	h. stayed
9. followed	i. confident	i. remained
10. excused	j. lower	j. cowardly

Insert the right word from column A into a sentence below:

1. _____ every moment of your life if you can.

2. The prince _____ himself and rode toward the castle.

3. You _____ where people love and care for you.

4. Often control _____ of sadness or anger.

5. When you have a bully, always be _____ and smart.

6. In the presence of royalty, you should _____.

7. Be home before the clock _____ 6 p.m.

8. The sargent yelled to his privates, "_____!"

9. The son _____ whatever good thing he saw his parents do.

10. Keep your _____ free from garbage.

Lesson 14
Comprehension Quiz/Discussion Questions

Directions: Students should copy the questions from below onto a sheet of paper and answer them in groups of two or by themselves. Then discuss as a large group.

1. What did Amazing remember?
2. What did she do to help her friend?
3. Did the Prince help Amazing?
4. Who did the prince want to marry?
5. What did Sir Milton say to the prince?
6. Did Cinderella get away or did her clothes turn to rags?
7. Why did Amazing cover her mouth?
8. Did Cinderella know what Amazing did for her?
9. What did Sir Milton call Amazing?
10. Does Prince Han Seng know the Prince? What word does his name remind you of?

10. Han Seng, Handsome.
10. Yes, they are friends.
9. Daughter
8. no, Not at this time.
7. Because she was so happy to finally have a family.
6. She got away
5. That Amazing is his daughter
4. Cinderella
3. Yes!
2. She screamed and pretended to fall
1. The fairy godmother's advice

Dialogue

- Sir Milton: Hello, I am Sir Milton. I am here to see the Director of Lost Persons

- Receptionist: One moment please. Let me get him.(goes into room and comes back)

- Sir Milton: My dear sir, allow me to present my papers. I have just married and want to adopt this child.

- Director: Just one moment. Did she say your name is Sir Milton. I have great news for you!

Discussion 14/ Journal Questions

What was some of the best news you have ever received?

_____

_____

_____

How did that news make you feel or change your life?

_____

_____

_____

What is one of the best things or messages that we can say to one another?

_____

_____

_____

Why is it so important to give each other good messages?

_____

_____

_____

DEVOTION 14: Adopted or

Getting What You Wish Because of The Lord, My Miracle

What it means to be adopted into God's Family

Lesson #14 – Adopted or Getting Your Wish – Just like Amazing was blessed and got her wish to be adopted, so God blesses us a lot too because He is a God of miracles (Nissi).

Think about this Theme: <u>There are Kingdom Blessings and Miracles</u> that God does to show his people how special they are to Him.

1. 1 Samuel 1:27 (Hannah was blessed because she knew God) I prayed for this child, and the LORD has granted me what I asked of him. If you have a special desire for God to do a miracle in your life, you better believe that He wants to do one.

2. 1 Chronicles 4:9-10 (Jabez was blessed because he knew God) And Jabez called on the God of Israel saying, 'Oh, that You would bless me indeed, and enlarge my territory, that Your hand would be with me, and that You would keep me from evil, that I may not cause pain.' So God granted him what he requested."

3. Daniel 6:22 (Daniel was blessed because he knew God) My God sent his angel, and he shut the mouths of the lions. They have not hurt me, because I was found innocent in his sight. Nor have I ever done any wrong.

God does miracles today because He is alive!

Child Testimony:

I believe in miracles! I believe because there are some areas in which I failed but God turned them around and made me a star. For example when I was 11 I had decided to write a short story for the school Academy Awards Junior Writing Contest. I was in love with dolls so I had written a story called, "My Barbie Doll Clothes". I sat in my seat at the awards ceremony, but my name was not called. Olivia was called, Barbara was called. Even a younger student than me was called, but though I was an A student. I had lost. That day, I cried. But quickly forgot all about it.

The next year, the school announced the contest again. I started praying about what I could write about and asking God for a winner. Then I was on my way home and a bee was irritating me. It was following me wherever I went, but I finally got away from it. So I decided to write a story called, "Me and the Imaginery Bee". This time I sat at the ceremony and my name was called. I won the trophy for "Most Imaginative Story." For me, it was a miracle because I had never take a writing course, and had only gotten the story done at the last minute. Everyone praised me, but I knew that without God I could not have gotten it done!

Since that time, God has done more and more miracles in my life. After I became an adult, I wrote a grant and won over $100,000 in Hong Kong to start a children's center. God is a miracle worker!

Life Application: Ask God to perform a miracle for you.

Drama: Act like you (or several of you) are in a storm. One or some people can act like they are the storm. Then one person rises up and says, Peace be still and the storm freezes.

Picture P

Directions: Color something on the two sisters' bodies.

www.ingramcontent.com/pod-product-compliance
Lightning Source LLC
Chambersburg PA
CBHW062047090426
42740CB00016B/3048